Jim Morgan's
Walla Walla Bing Bang
Book of Classic Music and TV Trivia

Jim Morgan's
Walla Walla Bing Bang
Book of Classic Music and TV Trivia

By Jim Morgan

Plus the Ink™

An imprint of Minus the Ink Digital Publishing Group

Jim Morgan's
Walla Walla Bing Bang
Book of Classic Music and TV Trivia

Copyright 2014
By Jim Morgan
All Rights Reserved

Cover design © Scott Richards

ISBN 978-1623390204 (paperback)

ISBN 978-1623390235 (eBook)

Dedicated to my parents who are at the root of my sense of humor; and to Lincoln the Wonder Cat, who so often sat in on the broadcast of these trivia questions.

Acknowledgements

I had thought about doing a trivia book for several years, but it wasn't until Julie Ellis-Behnke told me it was possible that I began to think about its fruition. Her guidance through this fascinating project is not possibly appreciated enough.

A very special thank you to Scott Richards, for designing the front and back covers and providing support which will make this book something that can continue.

Table of Contents

Foreward, by Jim Morgan

I don't know why I have always loved the time period between the early 50's through the 70's. I was born in 1964, and grew up in a town very much like Mayberry from "The Andy Griffith Show."

Perhaps because I grew up in a very Christian family (my father was a Presbyterian minister), I still to this day prefer the older songs and TV shows....maybe I appreciate the innocence of the era and the amazing cultural and social changes that happened in the 60's and 70's.

I've always loved music, and my radio career started in 1984 at WASU, the college radio station for Appalachian State University in Boone, North Carolina. I had a knack for it, and got a job right out of college at an oldies station in Fayetteville, North Carolina. Here I continued my love for classic songs of all types, from Big Band and Elvis, to the British Invasion, to the great rhythm and blues songs of the period.

That company transferred me to a radio station in Myrtle Beach, South Carolina in 1988, and I've been here ever since. It's hard to find oldies radio stations anymore, but Myrtle Beach is a retirement destination, and every year more and more retirees from all over the country move here to South Carolina. And guess what kind of music they like to listen to?

I was very lucky. I took a job at an Easy listening station in Myrtle Beach that played lots of oldies, and eventually, when that station was sold, took another job at another easy listening station in town. For over a quarter of a century, I've been blessed to be able to play the songs I love and live in a beautiful beach town.

The trivia question segments (and the prizes listeners win) are one of the most popular segments on my morning show. Eventually they became so popular we started doing them twice each morning. From playing instrumental TV themes, to a short (less than a second, in some instances) clip for "Name That Tune," to questions about the greatest actors and actresses and their movies and TV shows. People love the memories! I love old movies and find that listeners have amazing recollections about movies like "Casablanca" and "The Godfather." I'm working on a second book, all about classic movies and the people who made them. This will focus on a wider time frame, including movies from the 1930's to the 1980's, everything from "The Wizard of Oz" and "Casablanca" to "The Godfather" and "Jaws."

To this day I still get calls from listeners who heard the question, but had to get out of their car and missed the answer. Sometimes they just wanted to know if they were right, or were so intrigued, they just had to know the answer. And there is some amazing trivia about some of our favorite memories that people have never heard!

I have decided to compile some of the best into a book so more people who love that time period as much as I do can enjoy them. Perhaps you bought this book solely for your enjoyment, but try using the questions for contests at parties or long car trips. The questions bring back great memories, and some are truly amazing. Some questions will test your memory of the facts, and some questions will tell, as radio great Paul Harvey used to say, "And now you know...the rest of the story."

Of course I wasn't around to witness all this first hand, and there is a lot of rumor and misinformation out there, especially in the digital world. I have diligently researched as much as I can about each fact, but I can't truly vouch for the veracity of some of the answers. In those cases, it is likely it is true, according to the best evidence I could find. Indeed, there were several fascinating stories I didn't include because I just couldn't find enough facts to support the story.

So here we are. Enjoy, trivia lovers!

Jim Morgan

Morning host
Easy 105.9 and 100.7
Myrtle Beach, South Carolina

Section One:

Classic Music from the best era ever...the 50's through the 70's!

Q: Buddy Holly's number 1 hit "That'll Be The Day" was inspired by what famous John Wayne movie?

A: "The Searchers," from 1956. Buddy and his band mates had seen the movie and Wayne's world-weary "That'll Be The Day" became a catch-phrase for the young aspiring musicians. They eventually turned it into a song. It was the first big hit for Holly, and was the first song John Lennon learned how to play on the guitar.

Q: Only 3 Oscar winning actors have had a number 1 hit on the Billboard pop charts. One of them is Jamie Foxx, who won an Oscar for portraying Ray Charles in the movie "Ray," and hit number 1 on the pop charts with "Gold Digger." Who were the other two?

A: Frank Sinatra and Bing Crosby. Frank won an Oscar for the movie "From Here To Eternity," and had numerous number 1 hits, including "Something Stupid." Bing Crosby won an Oscar for "Going My Way" and hit number 1 with "White Christmas," among others.

Q: In 1963 16 year old Leslie Gore hit number 1 on the charts with a song that described a teen melodrama..."It's My Party and I'll Cry If I Want To" told the story about a girl named Judy taking Leslie's boyfriend at her birthday party! The saga continued with "Judy's Turn To Cry," which hit number 5. What was the name of the boy caught up in the love triangle?

Turn page for answer

A. Johnny. Both songs were produced by Quincy Jones, who discovered Judy singing at a hotel. One day Quincy took 200 songs to Judy's family home. When Leslie heard "It's My Party," she said to put that in the "maybe pile." It turned out that it was the only song out of 200 that both Quincy and Leslie liked. When it was released, it only took 4 weeks to hit number 1. So they rushed back into the studio and recorded "Judy's Turn To Cry." Leslie's chart success in the 60's led to her appearance on the "Batman" TV show, in which she played one of Cat-woman's minions.

Q: Only 2 actresses have won an acting Oscar and also hit number 1 on the Billboard pop charts...who are they?

A: Cher and Barbra Streisand. Cher, who won an Oscar for the movie "Moonstruck" and also hit number 1 on the Billboard charts many times with songs like "Gypsies, Tramps and Thieves" and "Half Breed." Barbra Streisand, who won an Oscar for "Funny Girl," has had several chart toppers including "The Way We Were."

Q: He was born Arnold Dorsey in India, but after changing his name to an 18th century German opera composer with 6 syllables...he would go on to become one of the wealthiest singers in the world, worth well over 100 million dollars....who was he?

A: Engelbert Humperdinck. After he changed his name, "Please Release Me" hit the top 10 on both sides of the Atlantic. His long career included major hits with "There Goes My Everything," "The Last Waltz" and "After the Loving."

Q: What famous singer was a direct descendant of Abraham Lincoln's great-great grandfather, Isaiah Harrison?

A: Elvis. He is also the 9th cousin once removed of Barack Obama. Also, Elvis was a distant cousin of President Jimmy Carter. Carter was in office when Elvis died August 16, 1977. Carter said the next day, "Elvis Presley's death deprived our country of a part of itself. He was unique and irreplaceable." Elvis is distantly related to Tom Hanks and Oprah Winfrey.

Q: John Wayne wanted what young female singer to star in the movie he was making, "True Grit," in 1969?

A: Karen Carpenter! The Duke was judging a talent show that featured a then unknown duo...Karen and Richard Carpenter. John had Karen read for the part of "Mattie," but the producers went with Kim Darby, who had more acting experience. Wayne didn't like working with Darby. He said she was unprofessional on the set and that he had no chemistry with her. He called her the lousiest actress he ever worked with.

Q: Johnny Cash was such a popular entertainer he ended up with his own TV show. In 1971, he introduced a new young singer in his prime time television debut. That singer would go on to win 6 Grammys and sold over 40 million albums...in fact his greatest hits album alone sold over 12 million copies. Who was he?

A: James Taylor. The Beatles signed James Taylor to their Apple label and released his first album. With the help of Johnny Cash and the Beatles, "Sweet Baby James" has become one of the most influential singer/songwriters of all time. George Harrison was so moved by Taylor's "Something in the Way She Moves" that he took the opening line and wrote a song called "Something"...which hit number 1 on the pop charts.

Q: It's 1959 in New York city...and the choir of Erasmus High School is performing. One young male choir member would go on to a singing career....and sell over 115 million records. Amazingly, a young female member of that choir would go on to a singing career as well. She would sell over 140 million records...who were they?

A: Barbara Streisand and Neil Diamond were in the same high school choir before they hit the big time. They teamed up for a huge duet in 1978 with "You Don't Bring Me Flowers Anymore" which was number 1 on the pop charts for 2 weeks.

Q: Jim Croce went to Villanova University before he scored 5 Top 10 hits, including 2 number 1's with "Bad, Bad Leroy Brown" and "Time in a Bottle." But while he was at Villanova, he was friends with another aspiring singer and songwriter, who would go to hit the top spot on the music charts with a song that would be number 5 on the Recording Industry Association of America's (RIAA) Top 365 Songs of the 20th Century. Who was he?

A: Don McLean with "American Pie." When asked what "American Pie" meant, McLean replied, "It means I don't ever have to work again if I don't want to."

Q: Which 1971 Carly Simon song was used in a commercial for Heinz Ketchup?

A: "Anticipation." In the commercial, viewers watched as the ketchup slowly poured out of the bottle onto a hamburger, while the song played in the background. Carly wrote this song while she was waiting for singer Cat Stevens to pick her up for their first date. It got up to number 13 on the charts.

14

Q: What was the biggest selling 45 single of the 1950's?

Turn page for answer

A: "Hound Dog/Don't Be Cruel," in 1956 by Elvis Presley. By the way, Elvis also had the biggest selling single of the 1960s ("It's Now Or Never" in 1960). Elvis' version sold about 10 million copies worldwide. It was his best-selling song ever. "Hound Dog" was number 1 on the US pop, country, and R&B charts at the same time and topped the pop chart for 11 weeks — a record that stood for 36 years. When Elvis performed "Hound Dog" on the Milton Berle television show, he was nicknamed "Elvis the Pelvis."

The song had been written by Jerry Leiber and Mike Stoller, who wrote monster hits like "On Broadway," "Stand By Me," "Charlie Brown" and "Kansas City." In 1952 they wrote "Hound Dog" for Big Mama Thornton. Mike Stoller took a European vacation in 1956 and was returning on the ill-fated final voyage of the Andrea Doria in which 52 people were killed. After being rescued, Stoller was met on the docks by Leiber who told him, "We've got a smash hit on Hound Dog." Stoller said, "Big Mama's record?" And Leiber replied, "No. Some white guy named Elvis Presley."

Q: What movie soundtrack holds the record for the most weeks at number 1 on the Billboard album chart?

A: "West Side Story," with an astounding 54 weeks at number 1, was the most successful album of the sixties.

The Elvis Presley soundtrack "Blue Hawaii" was the second most successful album of the sixties...it was number 1 for 20 weeks in 1964.

Q: Inspired by his favorite singer, Frank Sinatra, a young man began taking voice lessons. When his father was injured at work, he had to drop out of high school and take a job as an usher and elevator operator at the Paramount Theater in Manhattan. One day, Perry Como stepped into his elevator, and the young man stopped between floors and started singing to Perry. After a while, he asked if should continue voice lessons or keep his job. Perry said, "Keep singing!" and referred him to a local bandleader. He would go on to sell millions of records and even had his own TV show in the sixties. And to top it all off, his idol, Frank Sinatra, said he had the best "pipes in the business!" Who was he?

A: Vic Damone

Q: Only one U. S. Congressman has had a number 1 hit on the Billboard charts. Who was he?

A: Sonny Bono, whose song "I Got You Babe" topped the charts in 1965. Sonny wrote that song for his wife, Cher. He was elected to Congress in 1994, and served there until he died in a skiing accident in 1998. He was 62 years old.

Q: In 1964, a television actor had a number 1 hit on the pop charts with a song called "Ringo." Who was he?

A: Lorne Greene, who played Ben Cartwright on "Bonanza." He didn't sing, he just used his incredible deep voice to tell the story of a legendary old west gun fighter and a lawman. It was Lorne's voice that got him started in showbiz in Canada, working in radio and narrating documentary films.

20

Q: What famous entertainer turned down roles in the following movies?

"The Rainmaker" (1956), "The Defiant Ones" (1958), "Cat on a Hot Tin Roof" (1958), "West Side Story" (1961), "Midnight Cowboy" (1969), "True Grit" (1969), "Willy Wonka & the Chocolate Factory" (1971), "A Star Is Born" (1976) and "Grease" (1978).

A: Elvis Presley. He wanted to do many of those movies, but his manager asked for too much money.

Q: In 1957, The Everly Brothers hit number 1 on the charts with "Wake Up, Little Susie," a song about a couple who falls asleep at the drive-in theater. When they wake up, they realize they are "in trouble deep." According to the song's lyrics, what time did they wake up?

A: 4 o'clock am. This was the first of four number 1 hits for the Everly Brothers and was President George W. Bush's favorite song of all time.

Q: She started as a backup singer. Her voice can be heard on "You've Lost That Loving Feeling" by the Righteous Brothers and "Be My Baby" by The Ronettes. Her first recording as a solo artist was a song called "I Love You Ringo," about Ringo Starr. She would go on to sell over 100 million albums worldwide! Who was she?

A: Cher. She holds the record for being the oldest female artist to hit number 1 on the pop charts. She also won an Oscar!

Q: Karaoke singing is extremely popular in the Philippines. And they are dead serious about their karaoke. In fact, there have been a number of fatal disputes which arose because of the perceived poor renditions of a Frank Sinatra song. What Sinatra song has resulted in karaoke singers being killed?

A: "My Way," Frank's big hit from 1969. The New York Times estimated 6 people have been killed for singing it poorly. The song was taken off of many karaoke machines because of the deaths. The phenomenon is known as "The My Way Killings."

Q: Who did Frank Sinatra call the best singer in the world?

A: Tony Bennett. Frank said "He moves me. He excites me when I watch him." He's the singer who gets across what the composer has in mind and probably a little more." Bing Crosby also called Tony the best singer he ever heard.

Q: In 1959 a young man who just had a minor hit song wrote another song that he felt would be big. He offered it to Elvis Presley, who liked it, but all of the songs for Presley's next album had already been chosen. He then offered it to the Everly Brothers. They suggested he record it himself. He did, and it became a number 2 hit and launched a career that included six top 5 hits and two number 1's....who was he?

A: Roy Orbison...the song was "Only the Lonely." Roy and Elvis were good friends. Oddly, both died after having heart attacks in their bathrooms.

Q: In the popular 1970's sitcom "Happy Days," lead character Richie Cunningham, played by Ron Howard, would sing the lyrics to a Fats Domino song in reference to pretty girls he dated, or wanted to date....which one was it?

A: Blueberry Hill, which was a number 2 hit for Fats in 1956. Believe it or not, that song was written by actor Al Lewis, who was in "Car 54 Where Are You?" and who played Grandpa on the 60's TV comedy "The Munsters."

Q: Andy Williams was a great singer and TV host, but he also formed a record company called Barnaby Records. That label released songs from Ray Stevens, including number 1 hits "Everything is Beautiful" and "The Streak," as well as singles by Paul Anka, the Everly Brothers and the Osmonds. In 1970 Andy signed and released the first album by an unknown singer-songwriter. It flopped, selling only a few hundred copies. However, that singer would go on to sell over 20 million records and is also a best-selling author. Who is he?

A: Jimmy Buffet. It wasn't until his fourth album that he found any success. In fact he was getting ready to quit the business when "Come Monday" got up to number 30 on the charts.

Q: According to Wurlitzer, who made the iconic American jukeboxes for decades, what was the most played song on their jukeboxes of all time?

A: "Hound Dog" by Elvis Presley, followed by Patsy Cline's "Crazy" and "Old Time Rock & Roll" by Bob Seger.

Q: Crosby, Stills and Nash had a number 21 hit in 1969 with their first song "Suite Judy Blue Eyes." It was one of the songs they performed at Woodstock. Judy refers to writer Steven Stills' girlfriend, Judy, who was a famous entertainer...who was she?

A: Judy Collins, who had piercing blue eyes and had big hits with "Both Sides Now" and "Send in the Clowns." Collins and Steven Stills had been dating for a couple of years, but she was performing in a Shakespeare Festival and fell in love with actor Stacy Keach. Stills knew the breakup was inevitable, and wrote the song with her in mind. Collins was actually in the studio when the song was recorded.

Q: What singer, known primarily as a country singer, holds the record for the most songs on the Pop Charts without hitting number 1? He had 36 songs on the pop charts, but never a number 1.

A: Johnny Cash. He came close..."A Boy Named Sue" hit number 2 in 1969. It was recorded live in San Quentin prison. Johnny released 96 albums and 153 singles.

Q: Henry Deutschendorf, Jr. was born in Roswell, New Mexico, son of Henry John Deutschendorf. The Senior Henry was an Air Force Lt. Colonel who set three speed records in the B-58 and earned a place in the Air Force Hall of Fame. Junior would go on to have 4 number 1 hits on the pop charts during the 70's. Who was he?

A: John Denver. An avid pilot, he died at the age of 53 in an experimental plane crash in 1997.

Q: Who was the first singer to release a "Greatest Hits" album?

A: Johnny Mathis. "Johnny's Greatest Hits" became the second longest charting album ever! It sold over 350 million records, and stayed on the charts for a staggering 496 weeks...that's over 9 years!

Q: A guy by the name of Ross Bagdasarian was playing around with a tape recorder and having fun by speeding up the tape to make his voice sound higher. He ended up creating Alvin and the Chipmunks. But before the Chipmunks, he had a number 1 hit in 1958 with "The Witch Doctor," a song about a guy who goes to a witch doctor because the girl he loves doesn't love him. The witch doctor gives him a 13-syllable phrase to say that will make the girl love him....what was that phrase?

A: "Ooo, eee, ooo ah ah, ting tang walla walla bing bang."

Q: Paul Anka had dated former Mouse-keteer Annette Funicello when they were on the concert circuit together in the late '50s. He wrote a song about their romance that became a big hit...what was it?

A: "Puppy Love" which got all the way up to number 2 on the charts in 1960. Annette released an album of Paul Anka songs, but ended up marrying Paul's manager.

Q: In 1960, the Silver Strands were a singing group of U.S. Navy personnel serving on the U. S. S. Jason, based in San Diego. After the Navy, they changed the name of their band to The Thundernotes. Eventually they got signed to a record label who wanted them to change their name again. The label promoter was trying to find a new name when he spotted a box of dishwashing detergent, and named the group after it. They would go on to hit number 3 on the pop charts in 1963...who were they?

A: The Cascades. Their hit song "Rhythm of the Rain" was written while the lead singer was onboard the ship sailing in the north Pacific during a heavy rainstorm. He said the words just came to him as he watched the rain. Glenn Campbell plays guitar on the song.

Q: What famous rock and roll singer has his name misspelled on his tombstone?

A: Elvis Presley. Elvis was named after his father, Vernon Elvis Presley, and Vernon's best friend, Aaron Kennedy. On Elvis' birth certificate his middle name was spelled "Aron." It could have been a spelling mistake or perhaps it was to make it similar to the middle name of Elvis' stillborn identical twin, Jesse Garon Presley.

Elvis was a spiritual person and in the 70's he sought to change the spelling of his middle name to the traditional and biblical Aaron. He spoke about this to his father, who chose Aaron for Elvis' tombstone.

Q: Burt Bacharach and Hal David wrote a song that they thought had potential. They offered it to Ray Stevens, who turned it down. They then offered it to Bob Dylan, who also turned it down. Once it was finally recorded, it hit number 1 on the music charts for 4 weeks, and won the Academy Award for Best Song in 1969! What was it?

A: "Raindrops Keep Falling on My Head" by B. J. Thomas. It was the first million-seller for Bacharach and David.

Q: BMI announced the Top 100 Songs that had the most plays on American radio stations. What was number 1?

Turn page for answer

A: Here's the top ten:

10. "Georgia on My Mind" by Ray Charles
9. "Rhythm of the Rain" by The Cascades
8. "Baby, I Need Your Loving" by The Four Tops
7. "Mrs. Robinson" by Simon and Gar-funkel
6. "Sitting of the Dock of the Bay" by Otis Redding
5. "Can't Take My Eyes Off Of You" by Frankie Valli
4. "Stand By Me" by Ben E. King
3. "Yesterday" The Beatles
2. "Never My Love" by The Association
1. "You've Lost That Lovin' Feeling" by The Righteous Brothers.

BMI reported that radio stations had played "You've Lost That Lovin' Feeling" over 8 million times!!! Glen Campbell played guitar on this song. If you were to start playing that song and repeat it 8 million times, you wouldn't reach the end until 53 years later!

Q: What famous singing group took their name from a bowling alley?

A: The Four Seasons. Originally, the group had several names but settled on The Four Lovers. But after being rejected for a gig at the *The Four Seasons* bowling alley in Union, New Jersey, they decided to adopt that name. The Four Seasons had 60 Top 100 hits over a 32 year span.

Q: This famous singer, who also has done some acting, started off as a busboy at the famous Sands Hotel in Las Vegas, the stomping ground of the Rat Pack. Within in a few years, he became the youngest headliner at the Sands in history. Who was he?

A: Bobby Darin. When he performed there October 6, 1959, he was only 23 years old.

Q: "The Wonder Who" was a singing group that released 4 singles in the 1960's. However, they were a very famous and successful group under a different name. They were recording a cover of Bob Dylan's song "Don't Think Twice," but were having problems getting it right, so they changed their voices and recorded a comedy version of it as a joke to lighten the mood. That version ended up getting released and hit number 12 on the charts in 1965. What famous group released that song under the name "The Wonder Who?"

Turn page for answer

A: Frankie Valli and the Four Seasons

As this song slid down the charts, it passed by a Frankie Valli single (although the Four Seasons were on the record, uncredited) and the Four Seasons' "Working My Way Back To You," giving the same group 3 hits under 3 different names.

Q: The song "The Naughty Lady of Shady Lane" was a number 3 hit on the charts for the Ames Brothers. It was about a new lady in town driving everyone crazy with her "come hither glances at every Tom, Dick and Joe" and when "offered some liquid refreshment, never says no."

At the end of the song, the naughty lady's age is revealed...how old was the Naughty Lady of Shady Lane?

A: 9 days old. Dean Martin also recorded a version of this song.

Q: An anagram is a word or phrase in which the letters can be rearranged to form another word or phrase. For example, the letters in Clint Eastwood can be used to create "Old West Action."

The term "Lively Sprees" can be arranged into what famous singer's name?

A: Elvis Presley. When Elvis started performing with his legs and hips shaking, he got the nickname "Elvis the Pelvis," which he hated. In fact, one letter sent to J. Edgar Hoover said Elvis was a danger to the security of the United States because his "lively sprees" could rouse the sexual passions of teenagers.

Q: February 3, 1959 is known as "The Day the Music Died." Buddy Hollie, Ritchie Valens, and the Big Bopper were all killed when their plane went down in a snowstorm. Shortly after the news of the crash went around the world, an aspiring young rock and roll group changed their name from "Johnny and the Moondogs" in honor of Buddy Holly and the Crickets. What was their new name?

A: The Beatles

Q: What famous Carpenters song started off as the jingle from a California bank's television commercial?

A: "We've Only Just Begun." Paul Williams wrote the lyrics for the commercial for Crocker National Bank in 1970. Richard Carpenter saw the commercial on television, got together with Williams and finished the jingle as a song. With Karen doing vocals, it got up to number 2 on the charts. Paul Williams also wrote "Rainy Days and Mondays" and "I Won't Last a Day Without You" for the Carpenters.

Q: This famous musician, before he went on to a very successful solo career as a singer, got a late phone call one night from Frank Sinatra's record producer. They were recording a new song the next day and needed several acoustic guitar players. Our musician agreed and showed up at the studio the next day with his long flowing hair, sun tanned, wearing blue jeans and boots. All the other musicians were dressed more professionally.

When Sinatra got to the recording studio, he saw the new guy, and yelled "Get rid of that long haired *expletive deleted*." Our mystery musician started to pack up when he found himself standing eyeball to eyeball with *The Chairman of the Board*. Sinatra asked him, "Can you really play that thing?" Without saying a word, the guitarist sat down and played. Sinatra said, "You can stay." The song they recorded was "Strangers in the Night" and it hit number 1 on the pop charts. The young guitarist who played on that record went on to a solo career and recorded over 70 albums, selling more than 45 million...who was he?

Turn page for answer

A: Glen Campbell. After the recording session, Frank went to Glenn, stuck a wad of money in his shirt pocket and invited him to a party at his Palm Springs home that night.

Q: What Frankie Valli and the Four Seasons song was originally named after First Lady Jacqueline Kennedy?

A: "Sherry." In 1962 it was their first number 1 hit. It was originally titled "Jackie Baby." "Sherry" spent 5 weeks in the number 1 position on the charts.

Q: Legendary singing cowboy Roy Rogers had a famous horse named Trigger. He was called the smartest horse in the movies. Trigger was so famous he got to place his hooves in cement at Grauman's Chinese Theater. What famous singer has a guitar he calls Trigger, named after Roy Roger's horse?

A: Willie Nelson. When Willie was having his possessions auctioned off by the Internal Revenue Service for back taxes, he was afraid they'd auction off Trigger. And Willie had vowed, "When Trigger goes, I'll quit." So he hid the guitar at his manager's house until his taxes were paid.

Q: Elton John was huge star in 1976 and his concert tour of the United States was very successful. Elton said one of the highlights of that tour was meeting an Oscar-nominated actor who came backstage after a show. Who was he?

A: Cary Grant, who was 72 at the time. Cary was also a huge Elvis fan.

Q: What famous singer had a pet turkey named Bow Tie?

A: Elvis Presley. Elvis was an animal lover. Reportedly, at two years old, he cried for days when his pet rooster died. He had several dogs, including a poodle he gave to his wife Priscilla. At Graceland, Elvis had chickens, pigs, several monkeys, geese, peacocks and donkeys. While they were building a fence for the donkeys, Elvis supposedly drained the swimming pool and kept them there. His Australian fans sent him a wallaby, which he donated to the Memphis zoo. Most famously, he had a spider monkey named Scatter who was fond of drinking whiskey and engaging in numerous acts of mischief. Elvis loved taking him to Hollywood when he was filming. When Scatter died, there were rumors that a hotel maid had poisoned him after he bit her.

Q: Lulu had a big hit with the song "To Sir, With Love" from the 1967 Sidney Poitier movie of the same name. She was a huge star in the U. K. and even had her own TV series. In 1969 she married a member of an English singing group, but they divorced in 1973. That group sold over 120 million records...who were they?

A. The Bee Gees. Lulu married Maurice Gibbs. They remained friends after their divorce. In 2003, Maurice died of a heart attack at the age of 53.

Q: In 1952, this young singer was performing at a private party for singer Al Martino. A talent scout in attendance was impressed enough to get the young man an appearance on Jackie Gleason's TV show, which led to more TV appearances and eventually a music and film career. Who was that young singer discovered at Al Martino's party?

A: Frankie Avalon. By the time Frankie was 12, he had already been on TV playing his trumpet. In 1959 "Venus" hit number 1 on the charts for 5 weeks. That led to the beach blanket movies with Annette Funicello in the 60s; and he also was in "The Alamo" with John Wayne, "Voyage to The Bottom of the Sea" and "Grease."

Q: This famous singer was named J. R. by his parents. The initials didn't stand for anything and he didn't have a middle name. However, when he joined the Air Force he was told they wouldn't accept double initials....so he told them to put down John R. They did. After the Air Force, he would go on to sell millions of records and even host his own TV show....who was J. R.?

A: Johnny Cash. By the way, Cash is his birth name. He left the Air Force in 1954 and went to Memphis to audition for Sam Phillips at Sun Records, and the rest is history. "Ring of Fire" was the first country album to cross over and hit number 1 on the pop charts.

Q: In 1968, Johnny Cash proposed marriage to June Carter onstage. She was the love of his life and he had asked many times before. This time she said yes. They remained together until her death in 2003. During the 80s, Johnny found some old love letters to June in the attic. But they weren't from him. They were from another singer. He burned them. Who were those love letters from?

A: Elvis Presley. Elvis and Johnny were good friends. In fact, it was Elvis who introduced June to Johnny.

Q: What singer has 2 number 1 hits on the pop charts and 9 verified holes-in-one on the golf course?

A: Johnny Mathis. He was a star athlete in high school, playing basketball and running track. In fact, he was asked to try out for the 1956 Olympic team! He loves golf and hosts his own tournament.

Q: This singer started wearing glasses to copy his idol, Buddy Holly. However, after a while of wearing glasses he didn't need, his eyes adjusted to the lenses and he's had to wear glasses ever since. He's also sold over 300 million records....who is he?

A: Elton John. He is known for his eccentric glasses...and says he has over 250,000 pairs of them!

Q: At his funeral, friends and family members placed the items in his casket that had a personal meaning to them.

They included:

- 10 dimes
- Several Tootsie Rolls
- A roll of Wild Cherry Life Savers candy
- A ring engraved with the word "Dream"
- A pack of Camel cigarettes and a Zippo lighter
- Dog biscuits, so he could feed the dogs in heaven

Who was he?

Turn page for answer

A: Frank Sinatra. He always kept dimes with him after his son was kidnapped...he had to make phone calls from various phone booths to talk to the kidnappers and ran out of dimes. After that, he always had 10 dimes on him. Tootsie Rolls were his favorite candy, and he always gave his daughter, Nancy, her favorite....the Wild Cherry Life Savers. She slipped them in his casket. Former wife Mia Farrow put in the ring, and Frank was a dog lover...that's why the dog biscuits were put in his coffin.

Q: In the 1960s, a country singer got his own TV show and helped bring country music into the mainstream by having singers like Roger Miller, George Jones, Charlie Rich and Buck Owens on his show as guests.

Also on the show were comedy sketches with an early Muppet, Rowlf the Dog, created by a young Jim Henson. Henson was so grateful for his big break in show business that he offered the TV host a 40 percent interest in his production company.

Eventually, Henson sold the Muppet empire to Disney for $150 million dollars. However the singing TV host declined because he felt like he did nothing to truly earn it. He told Henson he deserved all the rewards for his own work. And he said years later he never regretted turning down an interest in the Muppets.

Who was he?

Turn page for answer

A: Jimmy Dean. He had a monster hit with "Big Bad John", acted in a James Bond movie, and built a breakfast food empire with "Jimmy Dean Sausage!"

Q: Eydie Gourmet met her husband, Steve Lawrence, when they were both booked onto Steve Allen's "Tonight Show." They got married in 1957 and stayed together until her death in 2013, fairly rare for a showbiz marriage. Eydie's cousin, a male singer, was even more successful than her. In fact, he had 3 number 1 hits on the pop charts and has written over 500 songs...who is he?

A: Neil Sedaka

Q: Dean Martin released his first single in 1946 and he was still making hits in the 1960's. In fact, as the Beatles were ruling the chart in 1964, he hit number 1... with what song?

A: "Everybody Loves Somebody." Frank Sinatra had actually released this song in 1948, but it wasn't a hit. It knocked the Beatles' "A Hard Day's Night" out of the number 1 spot on the charts, prompting Dean to send a telegram to Elvis Presley that read "If you can't handle the Beatles, I'll do it for you, Pally!"

Q: The two highest selling solo artists of all time in the U.S. are Garth Brooks and Elvis Presley....who is third?

A: Billy Joel, with 77 million units sold. Billy was once a successful boxer on Long Island, winning 22 out of 24 fights. He had taken boxing lessons because he was frequently beaten up by neighborhood bullies. In his 24th fight his nose was broken, and he decided to go into music.

All Elvis

Q: Elvis died August 16, 1977. The last song he ever sang for others was at Graceland. Some friends and family were there. The song he sang that Monday night was a hit by Willie Nelson....what song was it?

A: The last song he sang was "Blue Eyes Crying in the Rain," at home, playing the piano for family and friends on Monday evening, August 15th, 1977. That song was Willie Nelson's first number 1 song as a singer on the country charts and hit number 21 on the pop charts.

Q: In 1976, Elton John took his mother and father backstage before an Elvis Presley concert. Elton asked Presley to perform his favorite Elvis song, which he did. Elton said it was the greatest record ever made, and it changed the way he listened to music forever...what was it?

A: "Heartbreak Hotel," Elvis' first number 1 hit. Elton says he remembers the day his mother came back from the record store with "Heartbreak Hotel"....on a 78 rpm!

Q: Elvis had 4 favorite TV shows in the 1970's...name one of them.

A: He was a huge fan of "The Jeffersons," "Good Times," "Happy Days" and "The Flip Wilson Show."

Q: When Elvis was introduced to the daughter of a famous singer, he told her, "They call me the king of rock and roll, but your dad is the king of cool." Who was he talking about?

A: Dean Martin. Deana Martin says her father and Elvis were working on movies at Paramount. She said she was standing outside Dean's dressing room when Elvis came pedaling up on a bicycle. Dean came out and Elvis came over to say hello. Deana said she was goggle-eyed at meeting Elvis.

Q: At the time of his death in 1977, Elvis was the second best-selling recording artist of all time, second only to whom?

A: Bing Crosby

Q: Elvis was a huge movie fan. His favorite actors were James Dean, John Wayne, Clint Eastwood, Steve McQueen and Marlon Brando. Which one of those actors hated Elvis?

A: Marlon Brando strongly disliked Presley. He said, "It seems to me hilarious that our government put the face of Elvis Presley on a postage stamp after he died from an overdose of drugs. His fans don't mention that because they don't want to give up their myths. They ignore the fact that he was a drug addict and claim he invented rock 'n' roll when in fact he took it from black culture; they had been singing that way for years before he came along, copied them and became a star." Actress Rita Moreno dated Elvis just to make Brando jealous.

Q: Hoyt Axton was a singer who had a Top Ten hit with a song called "Boney Fingers." His biggest success was as a songwriter. He wrote "Joy to the World" and "Never Been to Spain" for Three Dog Night, "No No Song" for Ringo Starr and "Greenback Dollar" for the Kingston Trio. He also appeared on episodes of "WKRP in Cincinnati, "Bonanza" and "I Dream of Jeannie." His mother, Mae Boren Axton, also was a songwriter. In fact, she co-wrote a song that Elvis Presley took to number 1 in 1956...what song was it?

A: "Heartbreak Hotel." She wrote the song after reading a newspaper story about the suicide of a lonely man who jumped from a hotel window to his death. She showed the song to Elvis in 1955. It was his first number 1 song, and stayed at number 1 on the charts for 7 weeks.

Q: While the Beatles performed concerts all over the world, Elvis Presley performed only 2 concerts outside of the United States. They were both in what country?

A: Canada. Therefore, all of his concerts were in North America.

Q: Elvis gave his mother a pink Cadillac. However, it didn't come in that color. What color was the Cadillac originally before he painted it pink?

A: Blue. He had it custom-painted for his mother. Elvis bought his first Cadillac, a 1954 Fleetwood Series 60, which was the color pink. It was destroyed in a fire between Hope and Texarkana, Arkansas in 1955. In July of that same year, he purchased a new Cadillac Fleetwood Series 60 in blue with a black roof. Elvis had the car repainted pink by a neighbor. He gave the car to his mother, Gladys. However, Gladys Presley never had a driver's license, and Elvis drove the car for the next two years.

Q: According to Elvis, who was the best singer in the world?

A: Roy Orbison, who had a 3.5 octave voice. Between 1960 and 1964, Roy had 22 Top 40 hits with songs like "Pretty Woman," "Only The Lonely" and "Crying." Elvis said Roy's voice was the greatest and most distinctive he had ever heard. Elvis was a big influence on Roy and they were good friends.

The Beatles were also big fans of Orbison...his first tour of England was with the Beatles. When the Fab Four's manager asked Roy to tour England with the Beatles, he responded, "What's a Beatle?" Twenty-five years later, George Harrison would work with Orbison again, as part of the Traveling Wilburys.

Q: Worldwide, what was Elvis Presley's biggest selling single?

A: "It's Now or Never." In December of 2009 songwriter Aaron Schroeder died. He wrote over 2000 songs and Elvis recorded 17 of them. The New York Times reported that the song sold more than 20 million records and was Presley's best-selling single ever. Schroeder also wrote "Stuck on You" (1960), "Good Luck Charm" (1962) and "Burning Love" (1959), along with other writers.

Q: Elvis Presley held the record for having a song on the Billboard Hot 100 for 23 straight years. That record was broken in 1993 when what singer hit the Top 100 for 24 straight years?

A: Elton John. In 1975 Elvis arranged for his daughter, Lisa Marie, to meet her favorite singer for her seventh birthday. It was Elton. In 1978, Priscilla Presley arranged for Lisa Marie to meet her favorite actor...John Travolta.

Q: He was 7 years old when he first saw Elvis on "The Ed Sullivan Show." He later said, "I couldn't imagine anyone not wanting to be Elvis." In 1975 he released an album that has sold over 6 million copies. One year later, he played a concert in Memphis, and afterward, took a cab to Graceland. Even though it was late, he saw a light on inside. He climbed over a wall and headed to the front door...but was intercepted by security and thrown out....who was he?

Turn page for answer

A: Bruce Springsteen, who later said, "I remember later when a friend of mine called to tell me that he'd died. It was so hard to understand how somebody whose music came in and took away so many people's loneliness, and gave so many people a reason and a sense of all the possibilities of living, could have in the end died so tragically."

All Beatles

Q: Which of the ex-Beatles had the most SOLO top ten hits in the U.S.? Was it...

A. John Lennon

B. Paul McCartney

C. George Harrison

D. Ringo Starr

Turn page for answer

A. Believe it or not, the answer is Ringo Starr.

Paul McCartney has more if you include his post-Beatles group Wings, but Ringo actually had more solo U.S. top 10 hits. With songs like "Photograph," "It Don't Come Easy" and "You're Sixteen" (a remake of the old Johnny Burnett classic, with Paul McCartney playing kazoo on the track), Ringo had 8 top 10 hits!

As a solo artist, Paul McCartney had 6 top 10 hits, with songs like "Uncle Albert/Admiral Halsey" and "No More Lonely Nights." With his group Wings, which included his wife Linda, Paul had an additional 14 top 10 singles, and 6 that hit number 1 on the charts, including "Band on the Run," "Silly Love Songs," and "Live and Let Die" from the James Bond movie of the same name. Throw in duets with Michael Jackson and Stevie Wonder, Paul had 3 more top 10 hits, including 2 number 1's..."Ebony and Ivory," with Stevie Wonder and "The Girl Is Mine," with Michael Jackson.

John Lennon had 3 as a solo artist; George Harrison had 4.

Q: On February 9, 1964 an aspiring young English actor appeared on the Ed Sullivan show with the Broadway cast of "Oliver." Also on the show that night were the Beatles, in their first TV appearance in the U.S. He watched their performance from offstage and later said "I saw the girls going crazy and I said to myself, 'This is it', and I want a piece of that." He would go on to be the lead singer for a group that sold over 50 million records and even got their own TV show...who was he?

Turn page for answer

A: Davy Jones of the Monkees. Davy was a child actor on a British soap opera before leaving acting to be a horse jockey. He got back into acting which is how he wound up backstage when the Beatles made their American television debut. He died in 2012 of a heart attack at the age of 66.

Q: By 1965 the Beatles were the biggest act in the world and during their 1965 tour of the United States everyone wanted to meet them. While in California, they were invited to meet a huge star at his Bel Air home. The Beatles were excited, but John Lennon came away a little disappointed. He later said, "It was like meeting Engelbert Humperdinck." Who was he talking about?

Turn page for answer

A: Elvis Presley, believe it or not. When the Beatles came in, Elvis was sitting on the couch and the Fab Four sat down. There was an awkward moment and then Elvis said, "If you damn guys are just going to sit there, then I'm going to bed!" Everyone laughed, guitars were brought into the room and a jam session started. A few hours later, the Beatles left with gifts from the always-generous Elvis, including a complete set of Elvis records, a gun holster with a gold leather belt, and a table lamp shaped like a wagon.

Q: George Harrison's number 1 hit "Something," is the second most covered Beatles song ever. John Lennon and Paul McCartney called "Something" one of the best songs Harrison had ever written. It was covered by Frank Sinatra, Elvis Presley, Ray Charles, Andy Williams and over 150 other artists. What is the most covered Beatles song?

A: "Yesterday." Over 3000 different versions of this song have been recorded by other artists. "Yesterday" was voted the best song of the 20th century in a 1999 BBC Radio 2 poll of music experts and listeners. It was performed over 7 million times in the 20th century according to Broadcast Music Incorporated.

Q: Three of the biggest cultural influences on the 20th century were Frank Sinatra, Elvis and The Beatles. Elvis recorded three Beatles songs and Frank recorded one, but it was one of the Beatles' songs that Elvis chose. What was the only song recorded by The Beatles, Frank Sinatra and Elvis?

A: "Something," a song George Harrison wrote that reached number 3 in 1969. Elvis recorded "Hey Jude" and "Yesterday," as well. Sinatra called "Something" the greatest love song ever written.

Q: When Paul McCartney heard Simon and Garfunkel's "Bridge Over Troubled Water," he felt inspired to write a song like it. He did, and it became a number 1 hit for the Beatles in 1970. What was it?

A: "Let It Be"

Q: In 1964, Paul McCartney came up with the melody of a song that he felt strongly about...so strongly, he thought perhaps he had subconsciously stolen it from another hit song. George Harrison later lost a lawsuit because "My Sweet Lord" sounded too much like The Chiffon's' hit "He's So Fine." Paul didn't have any lyrics to his tune, so he made up some temporary lyrics while he played the melody for friends and associates to see if they recognized the tune. He called the song "Scrambled Eggs." After being convinced that it was truly his...Paul wrote the lyrics and the Beatles recorded it. It was a smash hit....over 3000 different artists have recorded it. What song was it?

A: "Yesterday"

Section Two:

Classic Trivia from the Golden Age of Television

Q: In 1954, during her junior year in college, a professor invited an aspiring performer and some other students to entertain at a black-tie party. Afterwards, as she was putting some cookies in her purse to take to her grandmother, a man and his wife approached her. He complimented her performance and asked about her future plans. When he discovered that she wanted to try her luck with musical comedy in New York, but didn't have enough money to get there, he offered her a $1000 interest-free loan. The conditions were that it was to be paid back within 5 years and that his name was never to be revealed. He also required that if she became a big star, she would help others attain their dreams. She accepted the deal, became a huge TV star and never revealed who helped her....who is she?

Turn page for answer

99

A: Carol Burnett. She paid him back and helped others anonymously achieve their goals. She has never revealed the name of her benefactor.

Q: What TV series was the first to broadcast a tape of a previously aired episode? In other words, what TV show gave us the first "re-run?"

A: "I Love Lucy." Desi Arnaz invented the re-run during Lucille Ball's pregnancy. During the second season, Lucille became pregnant with her second child, Desi Arnaz, Jr. The pregnancy was written into the show and the episode "Lucy Goes To The Hospital" was watched by more people than any other program ever at that time (1953). After the birth, Lucille needed rest, but Desi owed the network more episodes. He decided to re-broadcast episodes from the first season. Unexpectedly, those re-broadcasts were a hit in the ratings so Desi, for better or worse, is the father of the re-run.

Q: What was the name of the dog on "The Brady Bunch?"

A: Tiger! He was only in a few episodes of the first two seasons. The original dog that played Tiger was hit by a car and killed after 3 episodes had been taped. They found another dog that looked like Tiger who appeared in some episodes until midway through the second season, when he was mysteriously written out of the show. "The Brady Bunch" ran from 1969 to 1974, but Tiger's dog house remained on the set and visible for the entire series. The reason why? The backyard for the set of the Brady's home was made of AstroTurf, the plastic green grassy material they use in football stadiums. But one of the studio's lights had fallen and burned a hole in the AstroTurf, so they put Tiger's dog house over the hole to cover it!

Q: "The Simpsons" holds the record for the longest-running prime time cartoon. What TV show held the record until "The Simpsons" came along?

Turn page for answer

A: "The Flintstones," which ran 6 seasons. Mel Blanc, the voice of Barney Rubble, was also the voice of Bugs Bunny, Daffy Duck, Tweety Bird, Porky Pig and Foghorn Leghorn. In 1961, Mel was in a terrible car accident that left him in a coma for two weeks. His wife and son spent those weeks at his bedside trying to revive him, but got no response. Finally, one of his neurologists tried a different approach. He went to Mel's bed and asked Bugs Bunny, "How are you doing today?" There was a pause and then, in a weak voice, came the reply..."Myeeeeeh...what's up doc?" The doctor then asked Tweety Bird if he was there, too. "I tought I taw a puddy tat" was the reply. It took seven more months in a body cast for Blanc to recover. He resumed his career and kept working until his death in 1989. His gravestone reads "That's All, Folks!"

Q: On what TV show did Clint Eastwood get his big break?

A: "Rawhide," which ran from 1959 to 1965. It is the 5th longest-running Western TV series of all time. Clint got cast in "Rawhide" while he was visiting a friend at the CBS lot and a studio exec saw him. The exec said Clint "looked like a cowboy" and the rest is history. The longest-running Western series is "Gunsmoke," which aired on radio starting in 1952 and then moved to TV in 1955, where it aired until 1975. "Bonanza" is second with 14 seasons.

Q: There are only 3 actors who have starred in 3 successful prime time TV series. In this case, the term "successful" means the series lasted at least 3 seasons. One is Bill Bixby, who was in "My Favorite Martian," "The Courtship of Eddie's Father," and "The Incredible Hulk." Harry Morgan was in "December Bride," "Dragnet," and "M*A*S*H." Who is the other actor to have 3 different TV shows that were on the air for at least 3 years?

A: Michael Landon in "Bonanza," "Little House on the Prairie" and "Highway to Heaven."

Q: Some modern-era daytime soap operas started on radio. "The Guiding Light" was one of them. When the show was finally canceled in 2009, it was the longest-running soap opera ever. Combining radio and TV, how many years was "The Guiding Light" on the air?

A: A staggering 72...it debuted as a 15 minute dramatic series on radio on January 25, 1937. It moved to television in 1952 and played on TV screens for 57 years.

Q: When Sesame Street was being created, the producers were looking for an opening theme song. Before they chose the song "Can You Tell Me How to Get to Sesame Street," written by Joe Raposo, they were going to use another song he had written for the show. That song would later be recorded by the Carpenters and hit number 3 on the pop charts in 1973. So what Carpenters' song was almost the theme song for Sesame Street?

A: "Sing (Sing a Song)." Barbara Streisand actually recorded the song first, in 1972. Joe Raposo also wrote Kermit the Frog's song "It Ain't Easy Bein' Green."

Q: "Rio Bravo" was a 1959 western starring John Wayne, Dean Martin and Ricky Nelson. The producer wanted someone that teenagers liked in order to attract them into theaters to see the movie. Nelson had starting singing on the television show "Ozzie and Harriet." Howard Hawks said adding Ricky to the movie probably added around $2,000,000 in ticket sales to the box office haul. However, Nelson was not the first choice for the role of Colorado. Hawks first approached another actor/singer who turned the role down. Who was he?

Turn page for answer

A: Elvis, who really wanted to do the movie with Wayne and Martin. However, his manager, Col. Tom Parker, asked for too much money. Elvis was also approached to be in the John Wayne classic "True Grit" ten years later, but again Parker asked for too much money. The role went to Glenn Campbell.

While they were filming "Rio Bravo," Ricky Nelson turned 18. He got a birthday present from John Wayne and Dean Martin: a 300 pound sack of cow manure, which they then good-naturedly threw Ricky in!

Q: Michael Landon starred in three hit TV series: "Bonanza," "Little House on the Prairie" and "Highway to Heaven." He appeared on the cover of TV Guide 22 times, the second most number of covers of all time. Who has appeared on the cover of TV Guide the most times?

A: Lucille Ball, a whopping 39 times, almost twice as many as Michael Landon. Lucy was also on the very first cover of TV Guide in 1953. It cost 15 cents.

Q: What was the name of the cook on "Bonanza?"

A: Hop Sing, who was played by Victor Sen Yung, who served in the United States Air Force during World War II. Victor got his big acting break as the "number 2 son" in "Charlie Chan in Honolulu". He played that role in 11 Charlie Chan movies, but he was best remembered as the cook on the Ponderosa ("You stay for dinner! Hop Sing catch a chicken!") Victor really could cook...in 1974 he wrote "The Great Wok Cook Book." In 1972, he was a passenger on a plane that was hijacked...the F .B .I. stormed the plane and during the shootout, Victor was struck by a bullet in the back. He survived, but another passenger and the two hijackers were killed. The eulogy at his funeral was delivered by Pernell Roberts, who played Adam on "Bonanza."

Q: On November 26, 1974 an episode of "M*A*S*H" aired on CBS. In this episode Hawkeye blows his lid after 10 days of getting only liver and fish in the mess tent. He then places a takeout order from a restaurant in Chicago that he loves. Yes, an order to be picked up in Chicago and delivered to Korea....what was the name of the restaurant?

A: Adam's Ribs. Hawkeye placed an order for 40 pounds of spare ribs, a gallon of barbecue sauce (he forgot the cole slaw) and found a way to get them delivered. However, when the food finally arrived, injured soldiers arrived in the 4077th and he was dragged away from the table. There was no Adam's Ribs restaurant in Chicago, but for decades afterward, fans of "M*A*S*H" went to Chicago asking for directions to Adam's Ribs. In 2008, a struggling restaurant re-named itself Adam's Rib and Ale House to increase business.

Q: The great singing cowboy Roy Rogers was asked to make an appearance on a 70's TV show. He agreed, but only if the star of the show wore more clothing than she normally did. The producers agreed and Roy made his appearance....what TV show was it?

A: "Wonder Woman," starring Linda Carter.

Q: Speaking of "Wonder Woman," Linda Carter started her career as a singer. She has released 3 albums.

Before becoming a TV star, she was the lead singer of a band named The Relatives, who played at a casino in Law Vegas. The drummer in that band would go on to an acting career as well. In fact, he won an Emmy for his role on "M*A*S*H." Who was he?

A: Gary Burghoff, who played Radar O'Reilly. There are a couple of episodes of "M*A*S*H" where Radar is seen playing the drums.

Q: On July 1, 1956 Elvis Presley debuted on "The Steve Allen Show." That appearance helped his skyrocketing popularity. Another performer debuted on the show that night, a young comedian. He went on to become one of the biggest TV stars ever...who was he?

A: Andy Griffith, whose characters Andy Taylor and Ben Matlock made him famous. As did his comedy routine of Hamlet and of Elvis famously singing "Hound Dog" to a basset hound. Steve Lawrence and Edye Gourmet were also on the show.

Q: Johnny Carson hosted "The Tonight Show" for 29 years, 7 months and 21 days. That was the record for hosting a TV network series for the longest time until what TV show host broke the record, hosting his show for 35 years?

A: Bob Barker. He hosted "The Price is Right" from 1972 to 2007. Bob had a black belt in karate and earned a red belt in Tang Soo Do karate from Chuck Norris. Vanna White was a contestant on "The Price is Right" before becoming the most famous letter turner in the world on "Wheel of Fortune."

Q: Howard Hesseman is best remembered as playing disc jockey Johnny Fever on "WKRP in Cincinnati." He had been a radio DJ before becoming an actor. However, Howard was not the first choice to play Johnny Fever. The role was first offered to a former teen idol...but he turned it down. Who was he?

A: David Cassidy, best known for playing Keith Partridge on "The Partridge Family."

Q: Which two cast members of "The Mary Tyler Moore Show" were best friends BEFORE getting their roles on the show?

A: Gavin McLeod, who played Murray and Ted Knight, who played Ted. In fact, before the show, Gavin bought his first house in the same neighborhood as Knight. Gavin's acting career certainly had a nautical theme. He played Happy Haines on "McHale's Navy" with Ernest Borgnine and Tim Conway. He left that show to play the role of a sailor in the movie "The Sand Pebbles" with Steve McQueen. He was also in the submarine movie "Operation Petticoat" with Cary Grant. And, of course, he's probably best remembered as Captain Stubing on "The Love Boat."

Q: In 1977, ABC attached the first "viewer discretion advised" warning before what TV show?

A: "Soap," which would go on to be nominated for 17 Emmys. It was something of a nighttime parody of daytime soap operas. "Soap" had several controversial story lines; including murder, demonic possession and the first openly gay character on network TV (played by a young Billy Crystal). The TV show "Benson" was a spinoff from "Soap."

Q: Tony Dow played Wally on "Leave it to Beaver." He was born in Hollywood and his mother was a movie stunt woman. Before "Leave it to Beaver" Tony had almost no acting experience....instead, he was an athlete. In fact, he won a gold medal in the Junior Olympics....in what sport?

A: Diving.

Q: "The Dukes of Hazzard" ran from 1979 till 1985. Sheriff Roscoe P. Coltrane was played by James Best, who appeared in some big western movies in the 50's and 60's. "The Andy Griffith Show" fans may remember him as Jim Lindsey, the guitar player in a couple of episodes that joined Bobby Fleet and his Band With A Beat. James Best had a couple of cousins who were entertainers. As a duo, they had over 20 Top 40 singles on the pop charts...who were they?

A: The Everly Brothers. Best's mother was the sister of Ike Everly, father of the pop sensations.

Q: On the TV show "Cheers," you may remember the character of Carla getting married to a hockey player named Eddie Le Bec. Eddie was played by Jay Thomas, a Los Angeles disc jockey. One day Jay was doing his morning show on Power 106 when a listener phoned in and asked him what it was like working with Rhea Perlman, who played Carla. Jay said she was terrible to work with and he didn't like having to kiss her on the show! Unfortunately for Jay, Rhea Perlman happened to be listening and just a few weeks later, Eddie's character was killed off and Jay was never on the show again. How did the writers of "Cheers" kill off the character of Eddie Le Bec?

A: Although viewers didn't see it, Eddie was killed in a bizarre accident with a Zamboni, the big machine that resurfaces ice skating rinks.

Q: Which TV series included among its key cast members Roy Hinkley, Eunice Howell and Jonas Grumby?

A: "Gilligan's Island." Roy Hinkley was better known as the Professor, Eunice Howell was more often called "Lovey" by her husband Thurston and Jonas Grumby was better known as the Skipper. It is rumored that Gilligan's first name was Will, and had only been used once, on the never-aired pilot. However, creator Sherwood Swartz has said that Gilligan was the character's first name and no surname was ever given. Alan Hale loved being the Skipper. He owned a seafood restaurant called Alan Hale's Lobster Barrel in Los Angeles where he would greet diners dressed as the Skipper, with a big blue shirt and a white skipper hat!

Q: Gene Hackman was being considered for the lead in a TV show in 1968. However, the producers thought he wasn't famous enough and chose someone else. Later that year, Hackman was nominated for the Oscar for Best Supporting Actor. He was nominated again in 1971 and in 1972 won the Oscar for "The French Connection." He won a second Oscar for "Unforgiven" with Clint Eastwood. None of that may have happened if he had gotten the role on that TV show...which one was it?

A: "The Brady Bunch." Producer Sherwood Schwartz originally wanted Gene for the role of Mike Brady.

Q: James Garner starred in "The Rockford Files." He had a neighbor friend who was a famous movie star. Garner kept his yard neatly trimmed and mowed, but when he wasn't there, the neighbor would throw beer cans on his lawn. It took a long time before Garner figured out who was doing it. The 2 actors had appeared in a movie together in 1963. Who was the movie star who liked throwing beer cans on James Garner's well-manicured lawn?

A: Steve McQueen. Steve and Jim met while filming "The Great Escape." Both had an interest in automobile racing and were good friends. Jim lived down the hill from Steve, who liked to lob empty beer cans down the hill into Garner's driveway.

Q: Who shot J. R.?

A: 350 million people tuned into watch "Dallas" to discover that the character of Kristin Shepard, J. R.'s wife's sister, and his former mistress, was the culprit. 76% of TVs in the United States were tuned in after speculation all summer long, following the previous season's cliffhanger finale. As a side note, Linda Gray, who played the long suffering wife of J. R., was the aunt of Lindsey Wagner, who starred in "The Bionic Woman." Lindsey was scheduled to be a passenger on Flight 191 from Chicago to Los Angles in May of 1979, but felt uneasy about the flight and skipped it. It crashed minutes after takeoff, killing everyone on board.

Q: In 1972, Alan Alda and Loretta Switt started playing 2 of TV's most memorable characters...Hawkeye Pierce and Margaret "Hot Lips" Houlihan. They were in every season of "M*A*S*H" until it ended 11 years later in 1983. Only 2 other characters were in every season...which ones?

A: Klinger, played by Jamie Farr, and Father Mulcahy, played by William Christopher. Famous characters who didn't make it to the end included Radar, Trapper John, Henry Blake and Frank Burns. Characters who joined the show included BJ Honeycutt, Charles Emerson Winchester, the Third, and Colonel Sherman T. Potter.

Q: "Chico and the Man" star Freddie Prinze didn't know how to drive a car until his roommate taught him.

That roommate loved cars, and ended up being one of TV's biggest stars ever...who was he?

A: Jay Leno. He has over 100 cars and 30 motorcycles.

Q: In the sixties and seventies, if you had a hit record, it was pretty easy to get your own TV show. It happened for Johnny Cash, Sonny and Cher, Bobby Goldsboro, Glenn Campbell, Dean Martin, Mac Davis and many more. On one of those shows, McDonalds used a commercial to introduce the country to a new hamburger...the Big Mac. It has sold billions since. What TV show had the first Big Mac commercial?

A: The "Glenn Campbell Goodtime Hour" which ran from 1969 to 1972.

Q: What TV family lived in Walnut Grove, Minnesota?

A: The Ingalls. "Little House on the Prairie" ran from 1974 to 1982. Laura Ingalls Wilder wrote a series of books between 1932 and 1943 about a farming family in the mid-west. The population of the real Walnut Grove is 871. It is home to the Laura Ingalls Wilder Museum. The character of Charles Ingalls was ranked number 4 in TV Guide's list of the 50 Greatest TV Dads of All Time. The character of Nellie Olsen was ranked number 3 on TV Guide's list of the 10 Biggest TV Brats.

Q: Arnold Ziffle was a character on what TV show?

A: "Green Acres"...he was the pig! Arnold had appeared on "Petticoat Junction" before "Green Acres." Arnold was trained by the same man who trained Benji...when he died, the ashes of Arnold and Benji were placed in his coffin. Arnold was also the only cast member of "Green Acres" to win an award for the show. He won the "Patsy Award" in 1967, given to the best performance by an animal.

Q: What was the first children's toy ever advertised on TV?

A: On April 30, 1952, a commercial for Mr. Potato Head aired. It had been invented in 1949 and was first sold in 1952. They still make them today. The original price was 98 cents. They sold over a million the first year and Hasbro has sold over 100 million since. In 1953 Mrs. Potato Head debuted, followed by Brother Spud and Sister Yam.

Q: It really is best to see an Alfred Hitchcock film from the beginning. In 1951, a young female movie usher was working at the Warner Theater on Hollywood Boulevard. "Strangers on A Train" was being shown. A couple arrived after the movie had started and the young usher advised them that it was a wonderful film that should be seen from the beginning. The manager of the theater overheard this and rudely fired her right then. Years later, after becoming one of TV's biggest stars, she had star on the Hollywood Walk of Fame placed right in front of that theater. Who was she?

A: Carol Burnett. In 1969 Carol was also the first celebrity to appear on "Sesame Street," in the premier episode.

Q: Jean Stapleton played Edith Bunker, Archie's wife on "All in the Family" from 1971 to 1979. When she left that show, she was offered the lead role in a new TV series and she agreed to take it. Just before filming was to start, her husband died and she backed out of the series. That show would last from 1984 to 1996, longer than "All in the Family" and was one of the most successful TV series ever. The actress that replaced Jean Stapleton was nominated for 12 Emmy awards ....what was the show?

A: "Murder, She Wrote," starring Angela Lansbury as Jessica Fletcher.

Q: Les Nessman, the intrepid newsman on "WKRP in Cincinnati" had won several awards on the show. He mentioned them often...can you name them?

A: Les was a 5-time winner of the Buckeye Newshawk Award. He also claimed to have won the "coveted" Silver Sow Award, for reporting farm news and the Copper Cob Award, also for farm news.

Q: In 1972, a hit movie that had debuted in theaters 2 years earlier made its TV premiere on NBC. When the movie ended at 11 pm, the city of New York's water system suffered multiple overflow problems because so many people flushed their toilets at the same time.

What movie was it?

A: "The Godfather." It won the Oscar for Best Picture and Marlon Brando won the Oscar for Best Actor. Al Pacino, James Caan and Robert Duvall were all nominated for Best Supporting Actor.

Q: Which member of the cast of the TV series "M*A*S*H" wore the real army dog tags he was issued when he served in Korea?

A: Jamie Farr, who played Corporal Maxwell Klinger on the show. After appearing in the 1955 film "Blackboard Jungle," James served in the army for 2 years in Japan and Korea. Alan Alda also served in the army in Korea, but neither was there while the conflict was going on.

Q: Sonny Bono got into politics after he decided to get out of show business. He reached that decision after filming a guest spot on a 70's TV show. Sonny flubbed a line and one of the regular actors on the show blew up and asked Sonny what the *expletive deleted* was he doing there? At that point, Sonny realized he had had enough of show business. He eventually would be elected to Congress. What TV show was he filming when he quit show biz?

A: "Fantasy Island." Believe it or not, it was Herve Villechaize, who played Tattoo, who cussed at Sonny.

Q: What year did "Captain Kangaroo" start on CBS?

A: 1955. It ended in 1984, nearly 30 years later. Bob Keeshan, who was Captain Kangaroo, said he based the show around the relationship between grandparents and children. Bob was the original Clarabell the Clown on "The Howdy Doody Show." Keeshan was a Marine during World War II. He died in 2004.

Q: One of the actors on the great western "Bonanza" was a part-owner of the Bonanza Steak House chain, which also owns the Ponderosa steak house chain.

Was it:

1. Lorne Greene, who played Ben Cartwright

2. Pernell Roberts, who played Adam

3. Dan Blocker, who played Hoss

4. Michael Landon, who played Little Joe

5. Victor Sen Young, who played Hop Sing

A: Dan Blocker. He was 6' 4" and weighed 300 pounds, so it seems right he owned a steakhouse! Dan died in 1972 after gall bladder surgery. "Bonanza" lasted only one season without him. Hoss was a nickname. His real first name was Eric.

Q: Larry Hagman from "I Dream Of Jeannie" and "Dallas" was a struggling actor in 1959 when he met another struggling young actor in a Broadway play. They ended up renting apartments near each other. Of course, Larry would go on to be a huge star....his friend did as well, starring in 2 hit TV series...who was he?

A: Carroll O'Connor, from "All In The Family" and "In The Heat Of The Night". "All In The Family" was the number 1 ranked TV show from 1971 to 1976. The "Who Shot J. R.?" episode of "Dallas" was the highest rated television show in U. S. history. By the way, Larry Hagman directed several episodes of "In The Heat Of The Night," and delivered the eulogy at O'Connor's funeral in 2001.

Q: The "Great Rural Purge" of popular TV shows on CBS happened from 1969 to 1972. Network programmers wanted younger viewers, so they canceled many of their highest rated shows. One actor said CBS canceled anything with a tree in it! Some of the successful shows that got the ax were "Petticoat Junction," "Green Acres," "The Beverly Hillbillies," "Mayberry RFD" and "Hee Haw."

Oddly enough, in 1972, CBS premiered a show that probably was more rural than any of the ones they canceled. It was scheduled opposite the very popular "Flip Wilson Show," which had been number 1 for 2 years. It was also fighting for viewers with "The Mod Squad," another popular show. However, the new show beat both of those shows, leading to THEIR cancellation. In 1973 it won the Emmy for Outstanding Drama and stayed on CBS for a decade. What show was it?

Turn page for answer

A: "The Waltons." No one gave it a chance. In its second season "The Waltons" was the number 2 rated show.

Q: The original cast of the TV series "M*A*S*H" starred Alan Alda as Hawkeye Pierce. But another original cast member also auditioned to be Hawkeye. Producers liked him, but not in that character....they convinced him to take another role on the show. Who was he?

A: McLean Stevenson, who took the role of Henry Blake. His grandfather was Vice-President Adlai Stevenson. To research his role as an Army surgeon, he borrowed a medical book from Alan Alda. Months later, that knowledge came in handy when McLean happened upon a car accident. Using what he had learned from studying that book, he was able to keep an accident victim alive until help arrived.

Q: In the mid-sixties, many TV shows that were being filmed in black and white switched to color. For example, the first 5 seasons of "The Andy Griffith Show" were filmed in black and white and the final 3 seasons in color. "Gilligan's Island" and "My Three Sons" did the same. The last TV show that was entirely in black and white ended in 1968 after winning 15 Emmys...what was it?

A: "The Dick Van Dyke Show was the last show to have every season filmed in black in white. After 1966, all shows were filmed in color.

Q: Jack Klugman, Lee Marvin, Burgess Meredith, Telly Savalas, William Shatner, Elizabeth Montgomery, Charles Bronson, Carol Burnett, Robert Duvall, Peter Falk, Dennis Hopper, Ron Howard, Cloris Leachman, Leonard Nimoy, Robert Redford, Burt Reynolds and Art Carney all guest starred on what TV show?

A: "The Twilight Zone," which ran from 1959 to 1964. It was hosted by Rod Serling, who died from a heart attack at the age of 50.

Q: Leonard Nimoy's portrayal of the character Spock on "Star Trek" is now recognized as iconic. But he was not the first choice to play the role. Gene Roddenberry's first choice was already on another TV show...believe it or not...."The Andy Griffith Show!" What cast member of "The Andy Griffith Show" was offered the role of Spock on "Star Trek?" (Hint: it wasn't Aunt Bea)

A: George Lindsey, who played Gomer Pyle's slow-witted cousin Goober! Before the role of Goober, George had actually played a lot of tough guy roles. In 1965, he turned down the role of Spock.

Q: Florence Henderson was already successful in show business before "The Brady Bunch." In fact, she was the first female guest host of "The Tonight Show." But when she arrived to do her screen test as Carol Brady, there was no one there to do her make-up. So she went over to the adjoining studio where another NBC show was being filmed. She was seated between the 2 male stars of the show who were getting their make-up applied. Florence said neither one of those TV stars even acknowledged her presence and ignored her the whole time. Of course, she ended up winning the role of Carol Brady. Who were the 2 TV stars that ignored her?

Turn page for answer

A: William Shatner and Leonard Nimoy, who were getting ready for their day at work on "Star Trek." Florence Henderson's best friend was Shirley Jones, who played the mom on "The Partridge Family." Shirley had turned down the role of Carol Brady.

Q: In April, 1970, Congress banned the advertising of cigarettes on TV and radio starting on January 2, 1971.

The very last TV commercial for cigarettes was broadcast January 1, exactly one minute before midnight, when the ban went into effect....on what TV show?

A: "The Tonight Show starring Johnny Carson." The commercial was for Virginia Slims. (You've come a long way, baby!")

Q: Harrison Ford gave us two memorable movie characters...Hans Solo and Indiana Jones. Before both of those roles, he turned down a role on a TV series because he found one of the characters too offensive. That show was one of the biggest hits of the seventies....what was it?

A: "All in the Family." Harrison Ford was offered the role of Mike Stivic, also known as "Meathead." However, Harrison found the Archie Bunker character too offensive. By the way, Mickey Rooney was the original choice to be Archie Bunker. Also considered for Archie were Jackie Gleason and Tom Bosley.

Q: After "I Dream of Jeannie" Larry Hagman was offered roles on two new TV series...one was for a show called "The Waverly Wonders," about a high school basketball team. The other was to portray J. R. Ewing on "Dallas." Of course, he chose "Dallas," which became one of the biggest TV shows of all time. "The Waverly Wonders," scheduled against "Donny and Marie" on ABC and "Wonder Woman" on CBS, didn't have much of a chance. Nine episodes were taped, but only 5 were shown before the show was canceled. What former professional athlete starred as a basketball coach in the short-lived "The Waverly Wonders?"

Turn page for answer

A: Joe Namath. Joe also auditioned to be the first host of the game show "Family Feud," but Richard Dawson got the job. TV Guide called "Family Feud" the 3rd greatest game show ever, so Broadway Joe lost out on 2 huge hits. By the way, if you asked Larry Hagman for his autograph, he'd say "Sure! But you have to tell me a joke first!" But because people told him so many dirty jokes, he started asking them to sing a song instead!

Q: You may be surprised to learn that Bob Keeshan, Captain Kangaroo himself, served in the United States Marine Corps during World War II. He was a sergeant. One of the soldiers under his command also went to become an actor, a famous tough guy who ended up winning an Oscar for Best Actor. Who was he?

A: Lee Marvin, who won his Oscar for "Cat Ballou," but is best remembered for "The Man Who Shot Liberty Valance" and "The Dirty Dozen." He was a lifelong friend of Bob Keeshan.

QUICK HITS

Q: On the TV show M*A*S*H, what was the name of Klinger's favorite minor league baseball team?

A: The Toledo Mud Hens.

Q: On M*A*S*H, what was Hawkeye's home town?

A: Crabapple Cove, Maine.

Q: The first episode of this TV show came in 77th...dead last in the Nielsen ratings that week and was almost canceled. 8 years later, it was the number 1 show for the entire season. It received a record 111 Emmy nominations. What show was it?

A: "Cheers!"

Q: This aspiring actress was a ballet star. She auditioned for the role of Mary Ann on "Gilligan's Island," but lost out to Dawn Wells. However, she would go on to become a big movie star and sex symbol....who was she?

A: Raquel Welch

Q: Ed Sullivan had a rule...no lip-synching on his show. What TV actress was banned from his show because she lip-synched a song in her first appearance?

A: Mary Tyler Moore. She could dance, but she didn't think she was a good enough singer to perform live.

Q: This actor, who attended Wake Forest University in North Carolina, auditioned for the role of the Skipper on "Gilligan's Island." He didn't get it. But, he went on to win 5 Emmys....who was he?

A: Carroll O'Connor. Yes, Archie Bunker was almost the Skipper. Carroll dropped out of Wake Forest during World War II to join the Navy. They rejected him. So he joined the Merchant Marines.

Q: What character topped TV Guide's list of the 50 Best TV Dads of All Time?

A: Cliff Huxtable on "The Cosby Show." Ben Cartwright was second, Pa Walton was third, and Charles Ingalls was fourth.

Q: Only 3 shows have ended while at the top of Nielsen ratings as the number 1 show for the season...name them!

A: "I Love Lucy," "The Andy Griffith Show" and "Seinfeld."

Q: What female TV star was actually played by a series of males?

A: Lassie. All the Lassies were male dogs because female collies tend to shed more. By the way, there was never an episode of "Lassie" in which Timmy fell down the well.

Q: What TV star was known as "The Abominable Showman?"

A: Jackie Gleason. The character of Fred Flintstone was based on Jackie's Ralph Kramden from "The Honeymooners."

Q: David Letterman and Jay Leno had one of the biggest feuds in show business as they both tried to replace Johnny Carson on "The Tonight Show." But in the 70's, they were both writers for a successful sitcom.....what was that show?

A: "Good Times."

Q: In 2008, TV Guide ranked the sexiest men on TV of all time...who topped the list?

A: Tom Selleck, from "Magnum, P. I."

Q: Ringo Starr was a big fan and agreed to take a role on a popular American daytime soap opera, but changed his mind and backed out at the last minute...which one?

A: "The Guiding Light." In 1985, he accepted the role of Locke Walls. He was replaced by Jeremy Slate. "The Guiding Light" was the longest-running TV drama in history, broadcast from 1952 until 2009.

Q: What American TV show was banned from being broadcast in Saudi Arabia because it had a pig in it?

A: "The Muppet Show." Miss Piggy was not allowed to be seen in Saudi Arabia. Her full name, by the way, is Miss Piggy Lee.

Q: On the TV series "The Odd Couple," what were Felix and Oscar's last names?

A: Felix Unger and Oscar Madison.

Q: What was the name of the family dog on "My Three Sons?"

A: Tramp. "My Three Sons" is the second longest-running live action comedy in U. S. TV history. "The Adventures of Ozzie and Harriet" is number 1.

Q: What TV series started each show by "seizing control of viewers' televisions?"

A: "The Outer Limits," which was created after the success of Rod Serling's "Twilight Zone."

Q: From the smash hit TV show "Dallas,"
what do the initials in J. R. Ewing stand
for?

A: John Ross

Q: This actress' first TV appearance was in 1955 as Happy Hotpoint, the Hotpoint Appliance elf, in commercials that aired during "The Adventures of Ozzie and Harriet" show. She would go on to be one of TV's biggest stars ever...who was she?

A: Mary Tyler Moore

Q: What was the name of Gomer Pyle's girlfriend on "Gomer Pyle, U. S. M. C.?"

A: Lou Anne Poovey

Q: Before Johnny Carson became the host of "The Tonight Show," he was the runner-up for the lead role in a very successful sixties TV series....what was it?

A: "The Dick Van Dyke Show"

Q: On the TV show "Rhoda," a spinoff from "The Mary Tyler Moore Show," what was Rhoda's last name?

A: Morgenstern. "Rhoda" ended up with higher ratings than "The Mary Tyler Moore Show."

Q: What Oscar winning actor was offered the lead role of Steve McGarrett on "Hawaii 5-0," but turned it down?

A: Gregory Peck. Jack Lord became the guy who said "Book him, Danno!"

Q: What was the first letter Vanna White turned on "Wheel of Fortune"?

A: 'T'. The Guinness Book of World Records says Vanna is television's most frequent clapper, averaging 720 claps per episode....28 thousand times each season.

Q: Who was Johnny Carson's first guest on "The Tonight Show?"

A: Groucho Marx

Q: Before they were big stars, the following appeared on what TV game show?

Sally Field, Don Johnson, Tom Selleck, Burt Reynolds, Karen Carpenter, Richard Dawson, Farrah Fawcett and Steve Martin.

A: They were all contestants on "The Dating Game," which aired from 1965 till 1986.

Q: John Wayne dressed up in a bunny suit for what TV show?

A: "Rowan & Martin's Laugh-In," in 1969. "Laugh-In" was the inspiration for "Hee Haw."

Q: Priscilla Presley, after splitting from Elvis, was offered a role on a TV show. She turned it down. It became one of the biggest hits of the seventies. However, she accepted a role on "Dallas," which was one of the biggest hits of the eighties. What was the TV series she turned down?

A: "Charlie's Angels."

Jim Morgan's Walla Walla Bing Bang
Book of Classic Music and TV Trivia

Also available for

Kindle at Amazon (www.amazon.com)

&

Nook at Barnes & Noble (www.bn.com)